W9-CHF-029

Saint Catherine Labouré

Written by Sister Marie-Geneviève Roux and Sister Elisabeth Charpy

Illustrated by Augusta Curreli

Translated from the original French by Caroline Morson

Edited and adapted by Mary Cabrini Durkin, OSU
and Patricia Edward Jablonski, FSP

ÉDITIONS
DU SIGNE

*T*he **Daughters of Charity** *were founded in France in the 17th century by St. Vincent de Paul and St. Louise de Marillac for charitable works. St. Elizabeth Ann Seton founded the Sisters of Charity of St. Joseph's at Emmitsburg, Maryland, in 1809. Thirty years after her death, the Emmitsburg community formally united with the French Daughters of Charity. Today, the five provinces of the Daughters of Charity in the United States continue their ageless mission of service to persons in need in a spirit of humility, simplicity, and charity.*

Publisher:
Éditions du Signe
B.P. 94-67038 Strasbourg Cedex 2 – France
Fone: (0033) 3 88 78 91 91 - Fax: (0033) 3 88 78 91 99

© Editions du Signe - 2000

Text:
Sister Marie-Geneviève Roux
and Sister Elisabeth Charpy

Illustrated by:
Augusta Curreli

Layout:
Éditions du Signe

Translation by:
Caroline Morson
English edition © 2000, Daughters of St. Paul

ISSN 1275-5230
ISBN 2-7468-0048-9

Printed in Italy by Arti Grafiche, Pomezia

Have you ever felt lonely or worried?

This story is about a young girl named Catherine, whose mother died when she was only nine years old. Catherine felt very sad. But Mary, the Mother of Jesus, became her heavenly Mother.

Mary gave Catherine a special mission. She was to let us know that Mary loves us and will help us if we ask her to. Catherine also showed us how to put love into practice by helping other people.

Before you read Catherine's story, turn to the back of this book. There you will find an explanation of some words which may be new to you.

Mary taught Catherine to grow closer to Jesus. Mary and Jesus will lead you closer to God's love.

This little village in France, named Fains-les-Moutiers (pronounced Fayn-lay-mout-i-ay), had more cows than people!

There were a few large farms grouped around the church.

You could also see a big tower. It was the pigeon house of the Labouré (pronounced Lahboray) farm, with 600 pigeons!

Nearby were the stable, the barns, and the farmhouse where the Labouré family lived.

6

There were seven children in the family. But there were more to come. On May 2, 1806, Mr. Labouré opened the living room door and called, "Listen, there's good news! You have a new little sister!"

"Great! What are we going to call her?"

"We'll name her Catherine Zoë," Mr. Labouré answered.

"And when is she going to be baptized?" asked Hubert, the oldest of the children.

"Tomorrow, Saturday."

Mr. Labouré worked in the fields. Mrs. Labouré looked after the farmyard animals and milked the cows. She taught her daughters to milk the cows, too. She also did the laundry for her big family, all by hand. No matter how busy she was, she took the time to teach her children. She wanted to give them a Christian education.

The family was glad when two more babies were born, Tonine (pronounced Tohw-neen) and Augustus. But one day little Augustus fell off a wagon. He was hurt very badly and could not get well. He would always be disabled. Augustus needed extra special care.

Worrying about her baby Augustus and working so very hard made Mrs. Labouré sick. She died on October 9, 1815.

Catherine was only nine years old. She was very, very sad. She cried and cried. Then she remembered how her mother had prayed every night to Jesus' mother, the Blessed Virgin Mary. All of a sudden, Catherine jumped up and ran to the mantel, where there was a statue of Mary. She hugged the statue and said, "Now you will be my Mom."

Three years later Marie-Louise, who was twenty-three, wanted to answer the call of Jesus. She told her father that she wanted to join the Daughters of Charity. They were a group of religious sisters begun by Saint Vincent de Paul to take care of poor sick people.

"But who will take care of Augustus? Who will look after the farm animals?" Mr. Labouré was worried.

"Tonine and I will!" answered Catherine, who was twelve by now. Tonine was even younger.

The two girls got up very early every day. They took good care of Augustus. They went from the pigeon house to the stable and from the garden to the kitchen, doing their chores. They got the meals ready on time. Their dad was pleased.

Like all children, Catherine also loved to play or go for a walk in her free time. Her family teased her lovingly, calling her by her middle name, "Zoë," which means "life." Catherine was the life of the family.

Just before her sister Marie-Louise left for the convent, Catherine had the happiness of receiving her First Communion.

In the morning before starting work, and often during the day, Catherine liked to pray to Jesus. When she could, she went to the village church, which was very close to the farm.

One night Catherine had a fascinating dream. She told Tonine about it. "I was praying in the church. An old priest came to say Mass. He looked at me, and I felt like running away. Then he said, 'Someday you will meet me again. God has plans for you.'"

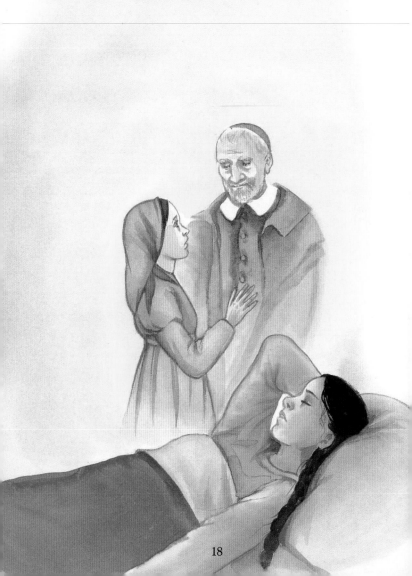

"I want to be a Daughter of Charity!" Catherine announced one day.
"Oh no! I've already given one daughter to God. That's enough! You won't leave here!" answered Mr. Labouré.

A few months later, Catherine brought up the subject again. "Dad, I would like to be a Daughter of Charity."

"That again? Never!" Her father was upset. "To take your mind off it, I'm going to send you to the city of Paris. You can help your brother Charles in his restaurant there."

With a sad heart, Catherine left Fain-les-Moutiers. Now Tonine would have to run the farm. Charles was happy to welcome his younger sister. But soon he realized how upset she was. Charles tried to speak to their father about this, but he wouldn't even listen.

Catherine's brothers talked things over. Hubert suggested that Catherine could come to the boarding school run by his wife. It wasn't far from Fain-les-Moutiers. There Catherine learned to read and write. She hadn't learned at home because of her mom's illness and death.

Catherine was excited to find out that there were Daughters of Charity near the school. As soon as she could, she went to see them. At the entrance to their house, she noticed a painting of a priest. "Who is that priest?" she asked.

"It's Saint Vincent de Paul, our founder," one of the sisters told her.

"He's the priest I saw in my dream!" Catherine exclaimed.

Hubert saw how happy Catherine was when she went to see the sisters. He decided to speak to their father again. Mr. Labouré finally accepted his daughter's vocation. He would let her leave Fain-les-Moutiers once and for all, to start her new way of life as a sister.

On Wednesday, April 21, 1830, Catherine entered the novitiate of the Daughters of Charity in Paris.

On the next Sunday, April 25, the people of Paris were celebrating. The body of Saint Vincent de Paul was being carried in a procession. The procession went from the Cathedral of Notre Dame of Paris to the Chapel of the Priests of the Mission.

A huge crowd was following. Catherine joined in, along with the other sisters. It was the feast day of Charity, which means love.

That night she saw Saint Vincent again in a dream. He told her about some terrible things that were going to happen in France. He also invited her to help people love one another.

In the novitiate the days went by, full of work, prayer and study. For about a year the new sisters prepared to become Daughters of Charity. Catherine was no different from the others.

Then something special happened. On July 18, a little before midnight, Catherine heard a voice. "Sister! Get up quickly!" the voice called. "Come to the chapel. Our Lady is waiting for you!"

"But someone will hear me!" Catherine answered.

"Don't worry," the voice encouraged her. "Everyone is sound asleep!"

Catherine got up and found a little child standing beside her bed. He was shining with light. She followed him to the chapel, which was all lit up. She waited there. She was a little bit afraid.

Catherine later wrote down what happened next. "Suddenly I heard a noise. It seemed that someone came to sit in the chair, but I wasn't sure. 'Here is the Blessed Mother,' the child said. Then I quickly knelt before her on the steps of the altar. I placed my hands on her knees. A long time passed, the most wonderful time of my whole life."

During this first meeting, Mary spoke with Catherine for a long time. She said that she would give her a mission. She warned her not to be afraid of the difficulties, but to come and pray to Jesus present in the Blessed Sacrament.

"When I went back to bed, it was two o'clock in the morning," Catherine said later. "I heard the clock chime, but I couldn't go back to sleep."

On November 27, 1830, Mary visited Sister Catherine a second time. Catherine explained, "It was time for evening prayer. I was in the chapel with all the sisters. I saw the Blessed Virgin standing there, offering to God the globe of the earth, which she was holding in her hands. Rays of light came out of her hands. They stood for the graces which Mary gives to people who ask her for them."

"Then I saw a sort of oval shape appear around Mary. This prayer was written in it: 'O Mary, conceived without sin, pray for us who have recourse to you.'

"The oval turned around and on the back of it I saw the letter 'M.' On top there was a cross with two hearts beneath. One was the heart of Jesus crowned with thorns. The other was the heart of Mary pierced by a sword. A voice said to me, 'Have a medal just like this one made. People who wear it, with trust, will receive many graces.'"

On February 5, 1831, Sister Catherine moved from the novitiate. She went to live and work at a home for the elderly in Paris. This house was in a large park. About fifty elderly people, who did not have much money, lived there. Seven sisters took care of them.

Since she was the youngest sister, Catherine was given the hardest jobs. She cooked and took care of the yard and the farm. She had good sense and experience from her work at home in Fain-les-Moutiers. She did an excellent job. She tried hard to prepare delicious meals to keep everyone healthy.

Even though she was so busy, Sister Catherine never stopped thinking about the mission which Mary had given to her. How was she going to do it without letting others know that she had seen the Blessed Mother? She wanted to be hidden from peoples' eyes. But she had to find a way to spread the message.

The Blessed Virgin gave her advice. She told her to talk to Father Aladel, a priest whom Sister Catherine knew well. At first he didn't believe her. But little by little Catherine convinced him and explained that Mary wanted the special medal made.

The first medals were finally made, in 1832, with the permission of the Archbishop of Paris. Father Aladel came in person to give one to each of the sisters at the home for the elderly. He admired how Sister Catherine stayed in the background. She received her medal without making any show.

In Paris at that time a terrible epidemic of a disease called cholera was spreading. Thousands of people were dying. A sister in Catherine's community was one of the first victims. It seemed that nothing could stop this plague. All the people could do was pray for it to end.

The Daughters of Charity gave the medal of Mary to everyone around them. They invited sick people to repeat the prayer which Mary had taught Catherine: "O Mary conceived without sin, pray for us who have recourse to you." Then surprising things began to happen! People were unexpectedly cured. Many turned to God.

This little medal which the sick agreed to wear was very quickly called the 'Miraculous Medal,' a name which would stick!

Just three years later, in 1835, one and a half million medals had already been made and spread throughout Europe.

Sister Catherine was now in charge of the nursing home section where the elderly men lived. She loved them all. If she had any favorites, they were always the most unpleasant or unfortunate ones. Once she was scolded because she had not punished some men who came home drunk. She explained, "No matter what they do, I can still see Jesus in them."

At the same time she was taking care of the elderly men, Catherine looked after the home's little farm. Besides the chickens and rabbits, she brought in cows to have fresh milk, and pigeons which reminded her of the ones on her family's farm.

She kept an eye on the garden, because the neighborhood children and the birds were always trying to steal the fruit. She kept the best fruit for the elderly people.

Even with all her work, Catherine prayed a lot. She explained, "When I go to the chapel I put myself in front of Jesus and I say to him, 'Lord, here I am. Give me what you wish.' If he gives me something, I am very happy and I thank him. If he gives me nothing, I still thank him, because I don't deserve more than that. And then I tell him everything that comes into my head. I tell him my sorrows and my joys, and I listen. If you listen to him he will talk to you, too, for with the Good Lord one must talk and listen. He always speaks when someone goes to him very simply."

At that time workers lived in terrible conditions. Many people were very poor, especially in the big towns. Some children as young as six years old worked in paper factories. These helpless children were also victims of alcoholism and violence.

The Daughters of Charity were worried about the future of the young people. They opened a school for the little ones and started evening meetings for the ones who had jobs.

This new project was part of the Blessed Virgin Mary's message to Catherine.

Mary asked that the sisters take care of the human and Christian education of young people. The sisters created an organization for doing this. This organization, called the Children of Mary, was set up in 1851. Catherine's niece became part of it.

While Sister Catherine was working and praying in the home for the elderly, the Miraculous Medal was spreading everywhere in France and all over Europe. "Where does this medal come from?" everyone was asking.

The sisters were wondering, too. "They say that it is our Sister Catherine who saw the Blessed Virgin," one sister whispered.

"That's impossible," another answered. "She's just like everybody else!"

Sister Catherine kept her secret and even scolded the sisters who talked too much. But she would always say firmly, "The sister who saw the Blessed Virgin saw her just as clearly as I'm seeing you."

"O Mary, conceived without sin, pray for us who have recourse to you." This prayer printed on the medal and repeated by millions of Christians was preparing people for an important event in the Church.

On December 8, 1854, Pope Pius IX declared the dogma of the Immaculate Conception. That means that Mary was filled with God's grace and goodness from the very, very beginning of her life. Four years later, in the French town of Lourdes, a girl named Bernadette was visited by a "beautiful lady" who said that her name was the "Immaculate Conception." Soon everyone knew that Bernadette had seen the Virgin Mary. But Catherine kept silent for forty-six years about her visions of Mary.

In July, 1870, France's ruler, Emperor Napoleon III, declared war on the country of Prussia. France lost that war, and the people rebelled against the Emperor. They set Paris on fire. The neighborhood of the home for the elderly was in the middle of the fighting.

54

The sisters took care of the wounded on both sides. Fighting men even invaded the convent. Catherine was arrested and taken to the police station. The police asked her to be a witness against a mentally disturbed woman who worked at the home for the elderly. This woman had caused many problems for Catherine. But Catherine refused to say one word about her. The judges were surprised! As a Daughter of Charity, Sister Catherine believed that every human being—even one who seems to be a troublemaker–has the right to be respected.

Catherine was getting weaker and weaker. She knew that she would die soon. She was worried because she hadn't finished her mission. Who would help her to have a statue made, showing Mary holding the globe of the earth? The Blessed Mother had asked for this statue. But Father Aladel, who had helped her before, was dead.

Catherine went to her superior, Sister Jeanne Dufès (pronounced Doo-feh), and told her about her conversations with Mary.

"You have received a great blessing!" said Sister Jeanne.

"I've only been God's instrument," Catherine quietly answered. "I'm not well educated. If Mary chose me, it was so that no one could doubt that the idea came from her."

Catherine continued, "Sister Jeanne, a statue must be made of Mary holding the earth in her hands. Just as a mother carries her child in her arms, so Mary presents to God all the life of the world. She invites us to love the world as Jesus loved it. She wants us to build a new world of love."

But Catherine was disappointed when the statue was finally finished. She remembered what Mary had looked like. "The Blessed Mother is much more beautiful than the statue!" she exclaimed.

In December 1876, Catherine was more and more tired. She didn't go out any more. She calmly told the other sisters, "I will not live to see the end of the year." On December 30 her condition got worse.

"Sister Catherine, aren't you afraid of dying?" asked Sister Jeanne.

Catherine shook her head. "What would I be afraid of? I'm going to see our Lord, Mother Mary and Saint Vincent."

The next day Catherine received Holy Communion. Then, while the sisters were praying the rosary with her, she peacefully died with a smile on her lips.

"There's no need to hide it from you any more, Sisters," Sister Jeanne declared. "It was Catherine who saw the Blessed Virgin and who received the mission of having the Miraculous Medal made."

"Once I saw Sister Catherine standing motionless in the chapel. Her eyes were fixed on the statue of the Blessed Virgin," remembered Sister Philomena. "I still think of her at that moment whenever I see the place where she was standing."

"I loved to say the rosary with her," added Sister Anne-Marie. "She taught me how to pray."

On January 3, 1877, a long funeral procession walked through the convent gardens. A large crowd had come. This funeral was a real honor for the woman who had always wanted to remain unknown.

Catherine was declared a saint by Pope Pius XII on July 21, 1947. Today you can see her body at rest in the Chapel of the Miraculous Medal at 140 Rue du Bac in Paris. Many people go there to pray. They do just what Mary invited Catherine to do when she said:

"Come to the foot of this altar. Here graces will be given to all who ask sincerely for them."

A few words to help you better understand Saint Catherine's life . . .

Chapel of the Priests of the Mission

The Priests of the Mission are trained in the spirit of Saint Vincent de Paul. (See the book in this same collection which tells about Vincent's life.) They are sent out everywhere to tell about the love of God, especially to the poorest among the poor. In their chapel, at 95 Rue de Sèvres in Paris, lies the body of Saint Vincent de Paul.

Children of Mary

A movement for young people. It used to be called the Association of the Children of Mary and is now called "Marian Youth." It exists in 60 countries and has almost 200,000 members.

Cholera

A very serious disease which is contagious and very often kills people.

Daughters of Charity

In the time of Saint Vincent de Paul, these were young girls and women from villages or farms who gave their whole

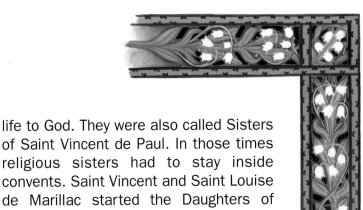

life to God. They were also called Sisters of Saint Vincent de Paul. In those times religious sisters had to stay inside convents. Saint Vincent and Saint Louise de Marillac started the Daughters of Charity and dared to send them everywhere. So they invented a new kind of religious life. The Daughters of Charity went out into the poor and sometimes dangerous neighborhoods, into the slums and hospitals to help the sick. They went into prisons and even onto the battlefields. Vincent said to them, "Your convent is the house of the sick. Your cloister is the streets of the town. Your chapel is the parish church." They were the first primary school teachers in the countryside, the first nurses, social workers, prison visitors, and special education teachers for children and young people in trouble.

Dogma
A truth of faith which the Church asks us to believe in.

Epidemic

Something harmful that very quickly affects a large number of people.

Immaculate Conception or "Mary conceived without sin"

Mary was chosen by God to be the Mother of Jesus and was filled with grace, preserved from all sin right from the moment of her conception, the very first instant of her life.

Mission

A project entrusted to a person.

Novitiate

The place of study and training for those who prepare themselves to become religious sisters, brothers, or priests.

Recourse

Turning to someone for help.

Vocation

A call from God, with a deep desire to belong to God.

68

Prayer

Thank you, Lord Jesus,
for the life of Saint Catherine.

She shows me how to be brave
when something is hard for me.
She shows me how to say yes to whatever
you ask me to do.

Thank you, Jesus, for the joy that you gave
Saint Catherine in seeing your Mother Mary.
Thank you for giving her the mission to make
our Lady better known and loved.
Thank you for the special gift
of the Miraculous Medal which Mary brought us.

Saint Catherine, please help me to treat others
with love as you did.
Pray for me to Jesus and Mary.

Amen.

If you are interested in learning more about
the Daughters of Charity
or other members of the Vincentian family,
we have included the addresses
of the five United States provincial headquarters,
as well as e-mail addresses.

DePaul Provincial House
96 Menands Road
Albany, NY 12204-1499
dcinfo@dc-northeast.org

St. Joseph's Provincial House
National Shrine of St. Elizabeth Ann Seton
333 South Seton Avenue
Emmitsburg, MD 21727-9297
office@setonshrine.org

Mater Dei Provincialate
9400 New Harmony Road
Evansville, IN 47720-8912
voc@doc-ecp.org

Marillac Provincialate
7800 Natural Bridge Road
St. Louis, MO 63121-4694
lgettemeier@dcwcp.org

Seton Provincialate
26000 Altamont Road
Los Altos Hills, CA 94022-4317
docdvoc@aol.com